THE FAR WOODS

SARAH BURWASH

I CANNOT INSTALL MYSELF ANYWHERE YET, I MUST CLIMB DIZZIER HEIGHTS.
BUT I STILL LOVE THE RELATIVE, NOT THE ABSOLUTE. THE CABBAGE
AND THE WARMTH OF A FIRE, BACH ON THE PHONOGRAPH AND
LAUGHTER AND TALK IN THE CAFES AND A TRUNK PACKED
FOR DEPARTURE. -ANAIS NIN

The Far Woods
© 2013 Sarah Burwash
Printed at Transcontinental Canada

Library and Archives Canada Cataloguing in Publication

Burwash, Sarah, artist
    The Far Woods / Sarah Burwash

ISBN 978-1-894994-76-7 (pbk)

    1. Burwash, Sarah 2. Artists' Books -- Canada. I. Title

ND249.B8597A4 2013   759.11   C2013-903718-7

I want to thank Arts Nova Scotia and the Canada Council for the Arts who have supported the creation of the work included in this book and have assisted me in travelling to multiple residencies, which have been incredibly impacting experiences and played a huge role in shaping this project. Thank you everyone at Sparkbox Studios, Elsewhere Studios, The Klondike Institute for Arts and Culture and Cabin-Time.

I want to thank my friends and family for all the encouragment. Thank you Lizzy, Jess and Janet for the adventure that brought us East and led me to meet Andy one sunny afternoon at Sappy Fest. Thank you Brenna, the big sister I always dreamed of having. Thank you Bree for critique and edits. Thank you MOLLY, for generously helping with scanning. Thank you Ben + Josh, my brothers, you guys have impacted me and my work in more ways then you could ever know. Thank you Mom + Dad, my guiding lights. A very important and special thanks to Andre, the sweetest guy I ever did meet who has been so patient, inspiring and loving.

And of Course, thank you Andy Brown for this oppurtunity and all your hard work.

Conundrum Press
Greenwich, NS, Canada

www.conundrumpress.com

Conundrum Press acknowledges the financial support of the Canada Council for the Arts and the government of Canada through the Canada BOOK Fund towards its publishing activities.

Canada Council   Conseil des Arts
for the Arts   du Canada

Canada

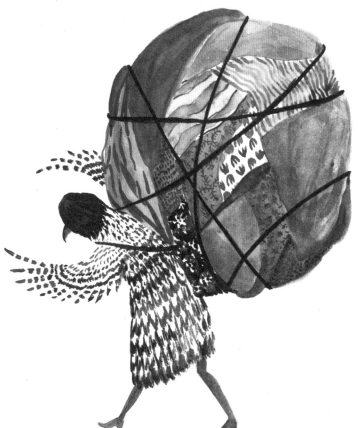

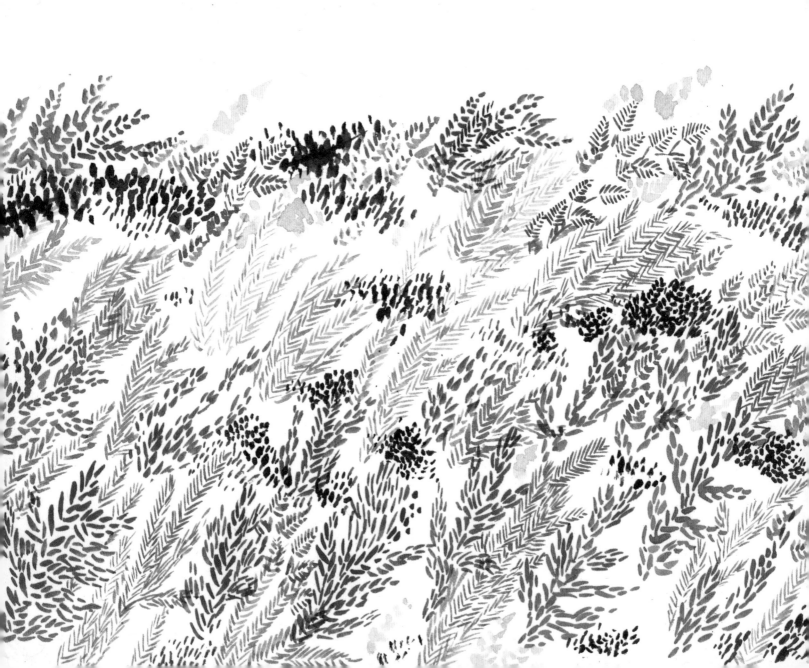

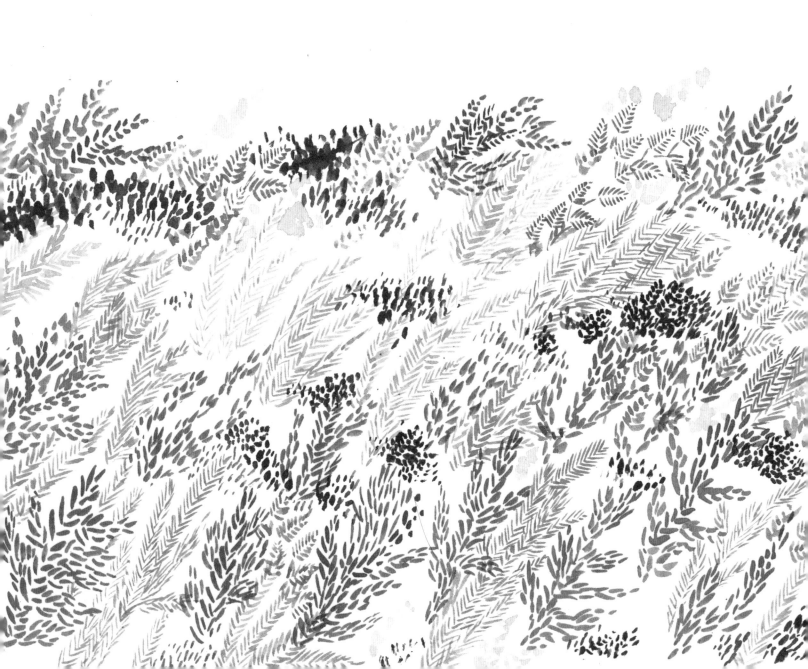

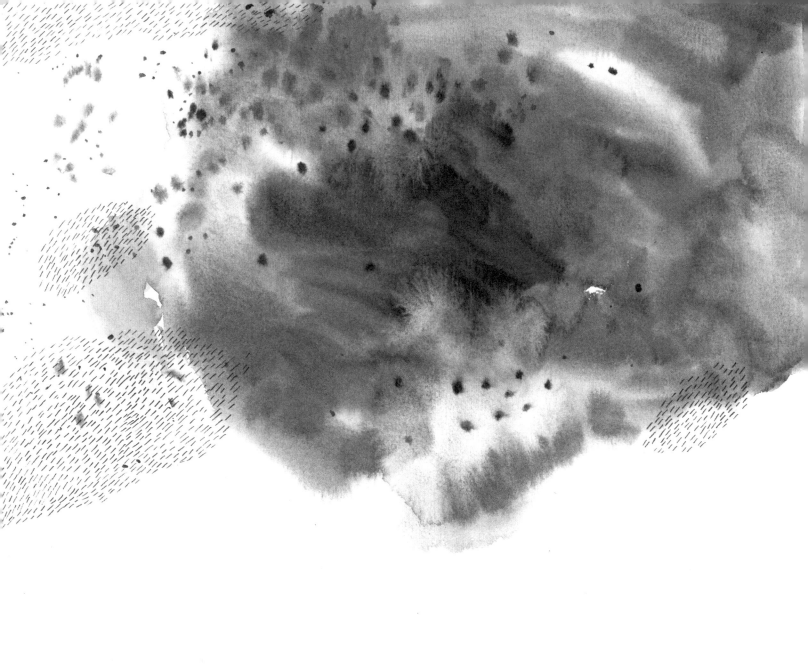

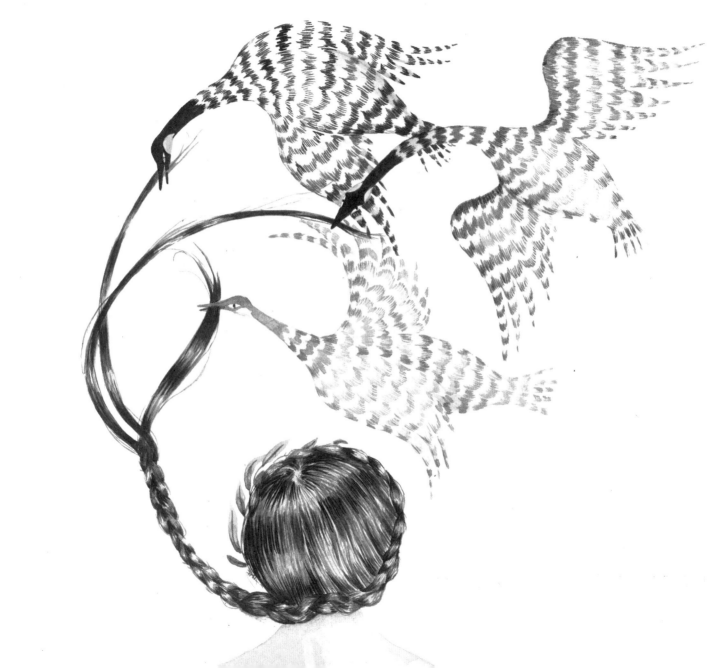

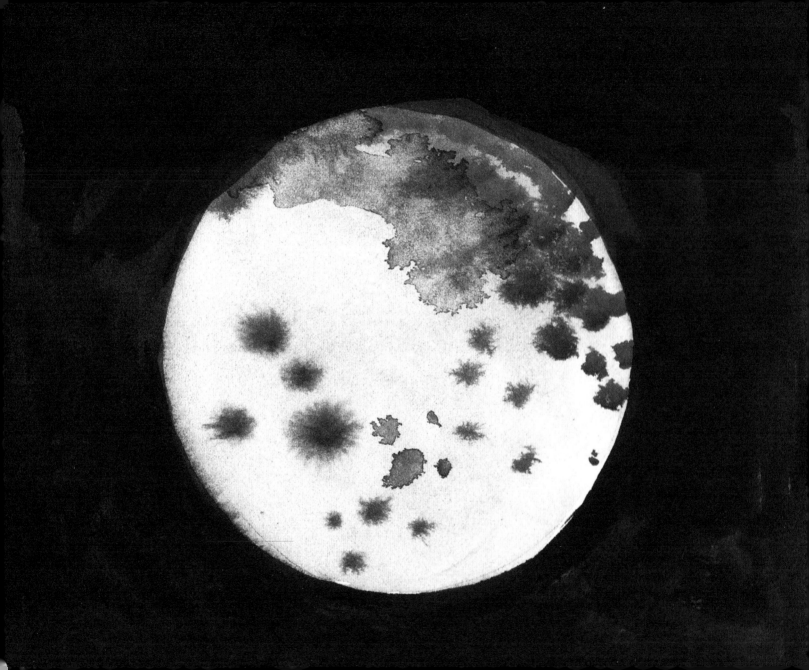